GROWING IN GRACE

GROWING IN GRACE

PHOENIX RIVERS

CONTENTS

1 Introduction   1
2 Chapter 1: Understanding Grace in Parenting   5
3 Chapter 2: The Christ-Centered Parent   9
4 Chapter 3: Establishing a Peaceful Home Environmen   13
5 Chapter 4: Discipline and Discipleship   17
6 Chapter 5: Nurturing Spiritual Growth in Children   21
7 Chapter 6: Overcoming Challenges and Obstacles   25
8 Chapter 7: Sustaining Grace in Parenting   29
9 Conclusion   33

Copyright © 2024 by Phoenix Rivers
All rights reserved. No part of this book may be reproduced in any manner whatsoever without written permission except in the case of brief quotations embodied in critical articles and reviews.
First Printing, 2024

CHAPTER 1

Introduction

Welcome to Growing in Grace! I am excited to share with you the culmination of my training and research on parenting from the unique perspective of the theology of the body. One of the gifts that brings the fullest potential of Dr. Gregory Popcak's resourceful book, Parenting with Grace, is the tandem dialogue of modern psychology and theology, emphasizing that Christian parenting is a ministry. Growing in Grace is an opportunity for the faithful to spend time delving into this rich Christian vision of love and human dignity and learn how to reach deeply within and transform their children through the power of Christ's presence in their lives.

Parents often ask me where to begin when making changes in their relationships with their children. Why did this book begin with a similar response? I offer you one simple place to begin in the work of peaceful parenting: take a look inside. In the following chapters, you will be invited to go deeper within to embrace personal self-inquiry and prayer as ways to center your decision-making on the lifestyle and attitudes of Christian grace. After working through the book, you will have allowed necessary time to sit with the scriptures, teachings of the saints, and the messages of your heart in pursuit of personal transformation. You will have equipped yourself with greater insights and tested tools to make peaceful parenting happen—action steps toward integrating your vocation as both a spouse and parent will only gain greater rewards: divine unity within the heart of your family.

Purpose of the Book

The purpose of this book is to help parents understand the heart of God and to delve into the nature of grace and how we experience God's infinite grace as He lovingly and patiently parents His beloved fallen children. Our aim, as Christian parents, is to help our own offspring grow in grace as they live and learn within our homes. We hope to impact the next generation and the lives of their offspring for Christ. Our prayer is to experience God's transforming grace in new, fresh, and unfamiliar ways as we walk out these sweet principles. Our aim is to lay out these principles in a plain fashion, drawing from a myriad of resources for peaceable parenting including Scripture, Christian authors and thinkers, professionals, and wisdom borne of hard-knocks experience. Most of what we say will be very simple... but very hard to do! We know all about that. Our aim is for you to be empowered by choice, motivated by love, and humble enough to allow God to break and renew you.

Our purpose is: 1. To draw parents toward a greater understanding of grace and to deepen a personal walk with Christ. 2. To help Christian parents understand the nature of their children, their God-given responsibilities, and how to adjust their attitudes and beliefs in practical ways. 3. To provide Holly's unique methodologies, which incorporate early childhood education, for the laying of a godly foundation in the home—one that is Christ-centered and is full of rich, deep knowledge as well as practical skills. 4. To encourage the parenting of intentional love, respect, and creativity in place of methods of position power and behavior control. 5. To enable young parents to compensate for their own parents' lack of grace in rearing and to provide for renewing love in Christ within their families.

Background and Context

Christ-centered, peaceful parenting is not just another parenting style or the latest parenting craze. Instead, it is an expression of the rich depth of the Christian faith lived in a familial context.

It is common for instructional parenting books, even those written for people of faith, to offer principles and ideas that can reasonably translate across a broad audience because they are observational or otherwise secular. While some principles of peaceful parenting could be viewed as such, the principles in this resource necessarily spring from central Christian doctrines: Christ's incarnation, death, resurrection, and ascension; the outpouring of the Spirit upon the Church; the gathering of the covenant community centered on the proclamation of the Word to partake in the Lord's Supper at the Table; the institution of kingdom-focused, grace-saturated relationships with parents and children—all bound together in the commandment to love God and love neighbor. This resource assumes this context, not as an afterthought because "oh yeah, peaceful parenting is more or less a Christian thing, too," but because isolated instructions in peaceful parenting strategies du jour are far less valuable and far less meaningful without them.

The growing community of Christ-centered, peace-minded parents in the Presbyterian Church in America (PCA) today will be the first to note that the concepts and best practices presented in this resource are not "new," nor are they "unique" in broader Christian contexts—particularly in those tribes and traditions who hold fast to the centrality of Word and Sacrament. What stands behind the resource is actually a collection of very old ideas, grounded in the received wisdom of the covenant community of faith as articulated through the Word, read and studied communally and under the preaching of the Word of the Lord. What stands out about the principles shared in this resource is not that they are new or unique, but that they bring together, in one relatively brief place, the core practices and perspectives expressed in Theological Frameworks, the Celebrate the Covenant Household and Family and Home Assemblies components of the Growing in Grace catechism curriculum. The principles are ancient. We think they bear repeating.

CHAPTER 2

Chapter 1: Understanding Grace in Parenting

The title of the book is 'Growing in Grace: A Christ-Centered Approach to Peaceful Parenting.' We plan to work on Chapter 1: Understanding Grace in Parenting. This chapter will primarily help the reader understand the concept of grace. The reader will be able to see what it is and to appreciate how showing grace nurtures and shapes the child in a positive way.

This section offers a brief glimpse into what Big S Grace is about. It will also convince the reader of the significance of understanding grace in parenting. Grace is, in essence, God's unconditional love extended to you. It is God's ability to cover you even when you are not doing things you are supposed to. Grace is unmerited favor. While it may not come 'natural' to all, its sweetness cannot be overemphasized. Grace fits in with nurturing and guiding young children. Showing grace early and often is an effective means to begin growth and grace. It also builds children who know no matter what happens, they will be safe. They have experiences to draw on that confirm love even when making mistakes. Grace covers.

Parenting is a journey aimed at guiding the child to become God-dependent. It is nurturing the child to connect to the God of the universe. He flows with unconditional love and will guide us to create love in our homes. Do we need to grow in understanding grace as we take this journey? We most certainly do. If real peace in our homes is what we desire, quietness, confidence and grace are what we need to consistently convey in upbringing. Christ 'raised the bar' many times as he conversed with people. Peaceful parenting is setting that bar - raising a new level of expectation on what children are capable of - what they will do when they experience a home filled with unconditional love and grace.

Definition of Grace

When we as parents look to our own faith, we can find ample resources to be the loving presence our children need us to be when we look to a compassionate Jesus – the Savior not of smiling, obedient mini-adults, but of messy, emotional, imperfect children. The kind of patient, compassionate, loving help that our faith calls us to provide to our children can be centered around grace, a concept that can often seem abstract. So let us begin by looking at the word more carefully – only by defining it can we understand how to live it.

First, grace is for real people – you, me, and our children, even when we do not behave our best. It is what helps us forgive and love when understanding or cooperating becomes frustrating. Grace is a make-up-your-mind lifestyle, and affects many aspects of how we live. It can help us hold on to children and stay connected during the tough times. Grace is an active verb, and in terms of parenting, it is love lived out in countless small, daily acts, sometimes behind the scenes. Pursue right living with your children, by infusing the relationships in your home with grace. It will help you to build your children's trust and respect, and in doing so, strengthen your connections.

Biblical Perspectives on Grace

With the expression of justice, wisdom, and love in the context of a relationship, grace is also one of the attributes of God. In the biblical and theological context, however, grace is eminently salvific. When the Bible speaks of grace, it usually focuses on two perspectives: 1) grace is closely related to God's covenant; and 2) grace is illuminated in the life and death of Jesus Christ.

One of the words the Old Testament uses to express the concept of grace is hesed, whose basic meaning is pity, mercy. To understand what grace signifies eminently to man, it must start from its application to God. Above all, its frequency illustrates the biblical belief in the initiative and active goodness of God that continually and at all times has raised the servants of the Lord. The root hsd in the active, and with vbm, is often used with reference to God in the Old Testament. In the great majority of the occurrences, Divine grace is meant in regard to Israel and individual members of the theocratic people. In the Psalms, Divine grace gratuitously gives the Midianites into Israel's hand. In the Arak narrative, it promises to deliver Arak into the hands of Gideon. The use of the noun hesed emphasizes especially, but by no means entirely, the quality of Divine grace which bestows gratuitous good where no obligation exists, and which is the resulting good. That resultant good often appears as help in distress, but the OT adds that it cannot be earned.

CHAPTER 3

Chapter 2: The Christ-Centered Parent

In my own reading, study, and personal experiences, I have identified several attributes and behaviors of a Christ-centered parent, which I would like to discuss here. I will nevertheless be the first to acknowledge that there are many other ways to parent with a Christ-centered approach—and that ours is but one of the innumerable successful possibilities. There are, however, many facets to a Christ-centered parent, a comprehensive list of which would exceed the necessary scope in this chapter.

This framework is based on our knowledge of the attributes and characteristics of Christ. As such, it shows that the parenting style should reflect the characteristics of Christ. A Christ-centered approach to life is based on Christ's principles rather than our own self-focused tendencies. It is characterized by radical love, which changes and refines our heart. It is not without struggle or affliction, but it shapes how we respond to the struggles of life. The life of Christ is available to us in every aspect if we seek to live it. It is not incompatible with being His disciples any more than any other area of our life. When those principles begin to take hold, Christ-centered parenting will have its basis in love that fulfills all law and morality.

Being gentle gives us the ability to correct others' ideas and behaviors with boldness, firmness, and truth. Although these characteristics and disciplines of Christ may be distinct entities, they are interconnected and dependent upon one another. This sort of self-sacrificing and service-oriented Christ-centered approach to life can only be pursued wholeheartedly. It is essential to be humble and willing to change. Our Christological tone should be supported by our own commitment to Christological devotion. Christ's grace and love are sufficient; we can do nothing without the Lord.

Imitating Christ in Parenting

The unique contribution of this book is its Christ-centered approach to parenting. Many parenting books imply or even instruct the acquisition of particular techniques or strategies as though children were pieces of freshly acquired Ikea furniture. Grace for any phase or situation is wiped out altogether, as though our principal need as parents is for more knowledge. Instead, Growing in Grace begins with considering the imitation of Christ as foundational to virtually everything involved in parenting. All of the chapters in Part 1 describe the behavior or qualities of Christ and then apply those to parenting. The intention is not to merely mimic the blessings of Christ in the hopes of winning our children, though love will always seek "the good" for them. Rather, the imitating of Christ is our fundamental posture of heart from which we can actually hope or expect any good to come.

And let's be clear, though not everyone would care, Christ is a man. So, what Mr. and Mrs. Baxter (or von Trapp) modeled in "parenting" Christ speaks and enacts to his disciples throughout the Gospels. This is music to the ears of Christian women for whom motherhood is part of what it means to become the best examples of those qualities while blessing others live and move and have their being every day. Likewise, it feels fitting that generations of ordinary men have cared deeply to take the heroes and anti-heroes of the Bible and history seriously when asking the serious question, "What makes a man?" This is not that book. This is the first of several growing in grace volumes.

Practical Applications

There are several practical points that could be added to this chapter. As with everything else in this book, remember that all practical counsel should be seen as an attempt to embody some facet of Christ's heart as a parent, which comes from being received in grace by Him. These are not things you "do" to present a certain image of yourself as a certain kind of parent; rather, they are ways to practice the being of a Christ-centered parent. All of these are good things the Holy Spirit can do in and through us. If we try to "do" them in a fleshly desire to change our "parenting image," they may multiply us on the outside. But on the inside, every effort to do something like this in our own strength shrinks our hearts, feeding our pride and our perceptions of this business instead of the hearts of our children.

In light of this, here are several practical ways to form a Christ-centered parent that we might look at later in this chapter: Treat our children as people, let and teach them to come to Jesus, pray for our relationships and leave them in God's hands, know boundaries are essential, parent from the spirit as a loved child following Christ, affirm personalities, teach self-discipline through invitation, but leave the design and the final outcome up to God, expect imperfections and forgive before they ask, don't major in the minors, have individual relationships with each child, always give honest answers, teach a theology of OCD, demonstrate forgiveness by asking for it and granting it. Can you think of any we're missing? Can you think of qualifications of any of these? Some have already been more proximately treated in the text of the book, and we can treat those less here.

CHAPTER 4

Chapter 3: Establishing a Peaceful Home Environmen

Families can become so entrenched in the chaos of undiscipline that they lose sight of the blessings—the peace and harmony—that follow close on the heels of an undisciplined lifestyle. The freedom, as well as the heart change, that cooperation produces enhances the serenity of life at an undreamed-of level.

Relaxed Today's children are relaxed. They haven't been raised with unnecessary turmoil and chaos. They were raised with a relaxed attitude, based on deep-seated Christian beliefs, which says, "A situation doesn't have to be perfect here for me to feel good." They have learned from experience that little things often are much ado about nothing, that they can let the unimportant go rather than let it anger or upset them. And in that rested, relaxed frame of mind, their whole behavior has changed.

With the general climate in their home being as tranquil as they can manage, parents stand a better chance of enjoying peaceful times of interaction and learning. Because children pick up attitudes from their parents, those most likely to raise peaceful offspring are parents by role-modeling peaceful behaviors and attitudes. Parents are responsible for establishing an atmosphere in the home. This includes maintaining a peaceful relationship with each other, and making an environment conducive to achieving peace in child rearing, as well.

Creating a Culture of Respect

To achieve harmony in the home, you must create a culture of respect, living with your family in a way that matters to you. Respect is living in the screening of appropriateness - asking "Is it disrespectful to do this?" or "Is it disrespectful to speak this way?" These questions guide our actions and our words. Respecting children is a two-way street. In our home, we want our children to respect us as their parents, and we want to show them respect in return. If you are a natural caregiver, you may thrive on caring for your children and they may in turn thrive in your care - but that does not inherently make for a respectful relationship. By cultivating mutual respect, you draw a boundary around your parent-child interactions, creating an environment that is safe, positive, and secure.

You will know you have created a respectful culture when parents respect children by: Communicating with children in a respectful manner while setting boundaries with respect, looking at children's feelings and behavior in the light of basic needs and brain model functions, and explaining the reasons for requests and rules, ensuring that the rules and interactions between family members reflect their level of development and individual uniqueness, allowing children an appropriate level of power to make real choices within areas of acceptable limits. It's okay for you as a parent to offer choices, but true power is involving your child in decisions that impact both of you.

Effective Communication Strategies

Communication serves to connect. The manner of communication often proves to be more important than closing the deal or winning the debate. In families, it is what holds us together and keeps us close. Here are a few communication principles informed by the Bible that I have found beneficial in my own family relationships. They will most certainly need to be adapted to your family and the specific difficulties you face.

1. Listen to understand. Practice repeating back what the other person says, clarifying when you got it wrong without defending your position.

2. Avoid emotional reasoning. Feeling something does not make it true. Learning to distinguish between thoughts, feelings, and behaviors helps form healthy, balanced interactions. This skill can be very beneficial to teach to children, too.

3. Practice assertive communication. Use "I feel/felt _____ when _____ because _____." Be specific about describing the event and how it made you feel. Avoid blaming the other person, generalizing, or using "you always" or "you never."

4. Control body language and tone to reflect genuine caring. Communicating love can have a significant impact on getting one's point across and encouraging others to speak openly, even if there is a disagreement. The goal of peaceful parenting is the nurturing of love and discipleship within the family. Effective communication should reflect these values, focusing more on the goal of understanding and maintaining a healthy family bond than any specific outcome.

CHAPTER 5

Chapter 4: Discipline and Discipleship

When we think about parenting, we have to think about two related ideas: discipline and discipleship. This chapter is really an exercise in examining peaceful parenting from that perspective; it's kind of a 30,000-foot-level picture of what we will begin discussing in greater detail about discipline next. So in this chapter, I hope to dig into the why of parenting—not just the practicality and fruit of parenting, but the purpose of raising our children up in the faith. There is so much to discuss when it comes to discipline and the Word of God, but I also want to make sure that I'm laying the groundwork for that discussion by planting truth about parenting first. That's what this is. Parenting 101 before a deep dive into what that means in practice.

An approach to parenting that I would label as Christ-centered, heart-based, and gospel-drenched, is concerned with both discipline and discipleship; it is always asking: How can I encourage heart change in my child by pointing out sin and pointing to Jesus? Sometimes, practical parenting "gurus" say we need to parent our children's behavior, not their hearts. We'll be studying all of this in later discussions on discipline, but I just want to highlight that even the approach we take to the wrong behavior of our children is both discipleship and discipline in action. Is this confusing? I hope not. I hope that we'll just find that, really, this approach is merely grace and gospel implications on repeat, always, in all things.

The Purpose of Discipline

If we are to assess whether or not we are doing a good job at carrying out our disciplinary actions, we would do well to first identify the underlying purpose that ideally guides a peaceful, Christ-centered parent. Jesus emphasizes that discipline is good, instructing us that "every branch that does bear fruit he prunes, that it may bear more fruit (John 15:2)." The main purpose of discipline, then, is to bear fruit. To use the terms of positive lifestyle discipline, the goal should not be putting our kids "in their place" but positioning them in Christ. Nor is it about "putting them in their place" as a self-glorifying parent or child, but about putting them in a place that is most beneficial for God's glory.

Put another way, the primary purpose of discipline is to realize the hope full of eternal consequences counted in Christ, which is the discovery of Christ's pure joy: a life "rich in love" and a "participation in the divine nature (CCC 1721)." Growing in peaceful discipline does produce positive behaviors from our kids. Yet those behaviors ought to be secondary to the primary purpose. They are, rather, a reflection of the "unwitting" spiritual lessons that have been learned along the way. The boy or girl who can intentionally control her emotions in anger has learned the virtue of temperance. The boy who involves himself in a task at which he is less-than-gifted has learned humility and the importance of persevering despite his ego. A disrespectful remark that requires no further disciplinary action might just be evidence that the child has taken the first of twelve steps in practicing true contrition. Each time we discipline our kids, we are forming them in the virtues - the same virtues the Greek philosophic tradition sought, though imperfectly, by way of reason. Our kids don't need to "know the reason behind" virtue (that's a neo-Kantian copout). They only need to know the subject of virtue: the person of Jesus Christ, who stands waiting for them at the end of their transformation in Him. In the words of C.S. Lewis, at which any life worthy of the human name should aim: "Jesus is the reason."

Discipleship in Parenting

Our children are prior to good behavior. Peaceful parenting invites us to nurture a richly grace-filled framework that restores the often anxious discipleship focus that premised the study. This section addresses the practice of Christian parenting that came into sharp focus of child-rearing. Parenting with a Christ-discipleship focus understands parents as primary disciplers of their children, or students who recognize the urgent necessity of being raised from the dead. As God pours his love into us, we discover who we are: image bearers and beloved members of Christ's body, even amid sin's wreckage. Shaped by this security, we non-anxiously invest in nurturing mutually edifying relationships with our children who are, after all, fellow amphibians.

Beginning from a restful space of being loved and being seen, peaceful parents are likely to have children who interpret as much in their disposition toward them, as well as in how they interact relationally. Rather than focusing on behavior modification, or pouring old wine into new wineskins, we remember we are here to cultivate perfect love, not just extinguish the bad behavior. We assume what is the most real thing about God and note what he has done in the truest sense. Then we become like him, extend him, and partner in planting the new lawn. Parents have an amazing opportunity and declare a powerful theological point every day. Not many of us sit around and discuss the doctrine of justification with our children; robust minds aside, we're more apt to talk about how we survive the chaos of the day and eke some joy out of our lives. Our daily practices declare what we really believe. The work we can do is to nurture in peace, to do the work of discipleship in the power of the Holy Spirit fostered within our children.

CHAPTER 6

Chapter 5: Nurturing Spiritual Growth in Children

From the very first day sin became actual, sin-scarred people fell into two different ditches in regard to children and spiritual things. One ditch is reflected by those who segregate "childhood religion" from that of adults. They want to tell Jesus to "pick on someone his own size," as they hide the real Jesus from them for fear that revelation might harm them. The other ditch reflective of the fundamentalist movement in the 20th century tends to strip "childhood religion" from adults because they do not want their children to pick up the same self-indulgent religious "novelties" they had so carefully set aside. Like throwing out bathwater, having discovered that the new interest has been a bit of a fad, genuine works of grace, they consider themselves "on the road to realization." As a result, that religion too has been pushed out of each converted home. Christianity has become an essentially adult thing, and only as "responsible" children can the little ones be true heirs of its treasures.

Our loving Lord, however, teaches something even the secular experts have discovered in recent times: Little children are not born mindless but are rather born mindful. And one point that captivates their minds is religious thoughts. We rob the smallest of their spiritual birthright if we do not bring those thoughts to where we can tell them they are ever at home. While people could decide to drop their heart-to-heart spirituality without serious problems, the faith of a parent in Jesus was never considered the private concern of a believer. Rather, the believer's faith was passed on to the heart and soul of the next generation as "the living flame-meal" of their present and future. Moreover, if we are constrained to admit that they already know precious little about the faith, what explains the failure of children to grasp the catechism? The reason is that they do not only catechize "children's hearts"; they also catechize "adult hearts." They address themselves not only to aspiring adults but to actual adults. And they write not for the religious philosopher, engaging in a religious discussion, but the ordinary reader, engaging in normal life. "Children's religion" is not the artificial product then; it develops beneath, nurtured and cultivated, the way a sugar beet forms under the growing warmth and light of the sun. If children, at the appointed time, do not cherish the gospel but leave the church to look elsewhere for interest, then the seeds of interest were never sown in the child's soul—not because we did not cater to so-called "age-appropriate" worship in music and scheduling, but because we did not cater to Christ. Rather, to children, always, must we minister Christ, who gave His all in love that we and our children might live.

Biblical Foundations

The Bible not only provides principles that parents can apply in childrearing activities, but it also offers the basis for the centrality of training children in biblical knowledge. Similarly, the Bible can be understood as a guide to undergirding understanding of the students' spiritual growth. Deuteronomy 6:4-9 highlights this component by advising parents to be conscientious about God's instructions at all times and to educate their children about biblical principles in daily life, both in the domestic environment and in communal life. Proverbs provides parents with motivation for training their children in the knowledge of the Lord, and God's faithfulness in sustaining His Covenant is also an inspiration for instructing the present and future generations in the knowledge of Him. The New Testament devotes much consideration to the responsibility of rearing children in the gospel.

Since the Scriptures speak of community discipleship and the teaching of children and youth, the child, as a fundamental unit in the life of a Christian family, is a focal point in the biblical story. Discipleship interventions to young people are grounded in the cornerstone of Christian religious life. Family initiates children into the religious framework, prior to corporate worship experiences with the entire church attending. The spiritual upbringing received from the family has a constructive or damaging influence on pupils at school and children's clubs. It deeply and rootedly impacts the way pastors are received in ministry settings. A family's objective is to provide spiritual influences on children in a church that shares similar doctrinal confidence and nurturing convictions. Even schools are compelled to teach the protection of children and methods of spiritual reform.

Practical Tools and Activities

- Singing with children: Children who develop a sense of joy in the sacraments of the Church stay with the Church much more readily. Theology is singing. We may also link a thematic association or song to home life. It is essential that parents take their child to church even at the cost of his running around or some minor annoyance because these church services have a positive, calming, blessing effect.

- Using sacred objects: Candles can act as a physical reminder of Jesus, especially His Ascension. People need reminders in order to connect with spiritual realities. It is useful in connection with bedtime prayers as the flame of the candle (that represents Jesus) is gradually extinguished. We can also use coloring-in books that represent a particular theme or church season and link to a story and the lighting of candles. The children may receive a small symbol or icon, participating in the liturgical life as sermons.

- Creative Kits: With these, the story can be told and made alive in the family's home, at a child's level. Bible stories can be 'acted out', first with verbal prompts and then as free-play. This is very powerful in integrating the child's hands and creativity with thoughts, emotions, and prayerful communication. Interesting games are linked to favorite bible stories familiar from church. Popular saints and miracle stories can be introduced but are in no way mandatory. Feeding the poor or stories of contemporary needs can also be introduced. Interviewing a saint can be invaluable.

CHAPTER 7

Chapter 6: Overcoming Challenges and Obstacles

Perhaps you are reading this book because you have taken an honest look at your parenting and you are discouraged with the results. Your "issues" may be more internal, and you struggle with anger, resentment, bitterness, or insecurity. Likely, it is a combination of timeless trouble and obstacles made possible by the 21st century. Either way, please know you are encouraged to persevere in this Christ-centered and peaceful way. Parenting was and is a daunting challenge, and it has always required the grace of God, the love of Christ, the help of the Holy Spirit, and the help and support of His people.

In this chapter, we plan to discuss the atheist at the PTA meeting, the apathetic spouse, and the pessimistic friend. We will talk about sibling rivalry, kids hating our food, and never getting to sleep through the night. We will discuss inconsistencies with healthcare plans and opposition from confused family members. We will chat about temper tantrums at Target, your job, and as you eat dinner with people who do not have children—or with your spouse on a rare date night alone! We will chat about folks who tell us we are damaging our children by not making them eat peas and friends who say we could make everything look good because life on Instagram looks fairy-tale perfect.

Dealing with Anger and Frustration

Teach me to side with my children in their quest for self-expression, with an eye always to behavior and relationships that are honoring to you. Grant me patience and a sense of humor. When I find myself becoming angry or frustrated, guide me to a sense of calm well-being that ought to be present whenever I am in your will. Reveal my shortcomings at a pace I can handle so that I might in turn be forgiving and understanding toward my children and their steps toward mornings of peace in our home.

As God's peace fills our home and permeates my feelings, my parenting will not be diminished but will instead become even more powerful, more full of grace and love. God, give me the grace to grow in this grace. Amen.

Like it or not, our children are exposed to our anger, irritations, disappointments, and frustrations. Sometimes we convince ourselves that they do not know, but they often do... or at least they do more than we think is good for them. The best way to teach our children to live calm and moderate lives in a world fraught with emotion is to be calm and moderate with them when emotions test us. It's not real fatherhood until it's fifth-year fatherhood. The fifth-year father begins teaching his children to have that kind of peace in their life, and they have to have somebody show them how to do it. I will never be the changing, temperate father that will teach my children peace until I am at peace. Before that, we all decompensate and choose our own obsessions to bring ourselves back to homeostasis until we are whole again.

Handling Difficult Situations

The dominoes fall quickly. A disagreement breaks out between three of four children. Before I can intervene, harsh words are spoken. Emotions run high. One child shoves another, who falls back into a snow-covered ditch. Down she goes. As I retreat to gather my thoughts, I simply say, "I can't have you this close to the road with cars coming. We need to move for your safety." I can't recall everything I said next, but I'm guessing much of it wasn't helpful. It may have been accurate, but it wasn't helpful. Once again, I lost my composure and made a difficult situation more difficult with my lack of grace and peace.

We promise our children they can trust us, but what we promise means very little when the pressure is on and we are in the driver's seat of chaos. So, what does a Christ-centered, peaceful approach to parenting look like when we're leaning back in the seat and holding the steering wheel at 10 and 2, convinced a cliff looms ahead? For this issue, we called upon several seasoned parents and those who work with children to provide practical ways we can grow in grace and peace when parenting life gets tough, revealing the peace of Christ through how we parent.

CHAPTER 8

Chapter 7: Sustaining Grace in Parenting

Spread the word: The mission of this book is to help parents adopt a Christ-centered, grace-based mindset on daily parenting matters. The overarching goal is to draw just a little closer to Jesus in their relationships with their kids. Even though a frustrating or difficult interchange may occur, the goal is for your love for your child to persevere, that is, to endure and be constant, even when you're upset with her behavior. This love isn't based solely on your feelings for your child (which, let's face it, can change a lot), but on a deeper principle that comes from understanding God's unchanging love for you. You know He loves you, bad choices and all, so that makes you love your child with a persevering love.

Idea #4: Stay anchored in grace. My hope for parents is simple: that grace will be the North Star of their parenting journey. If you have grace firmly anchored in your heart, it can guide the way you interact with your children. Early on in the parenting journey, we considered the devastating price we pay when we allow law—instead of grace—to rule our interactions with our kids. In this chapter, we want to loop back to that subject, this time considering how difficult it can be to introduce and then cling to a law-backing, grace-backed mindset, even as we walk deeper into everyday parenting concerns. We want to discuss some of the ways we are prone to slip into a graceless mindset, and the ideas for focusing on how we can continue to cling to the grace we have in Christ during times that are hard—not just when the sun is shining bright.

Self-Care for Parents

Grace-centered parenting is Christ-centered parenting. Christ's redemption and grace pave the way for our own future parenting. Because of what Christ has done and continues to do in our and our children's lives, we can train our children in the nurture and admonition of the Lord and parent from a place of peace, knowing that Jesus is our perfect substitute, fulfilled every aspect of the law on our behalf, and lived the perfect life we could not live. All of our children's failures and high, holy standards are already fulfilled in Jesus, and because of this reality, we get to parent with an unshakable peace that goes beyond our understanding. We get to parent with a gospel foundation and freedom from our moral record. We get to parent in freedom through grace.

I don't believe that any worthy list of self-care for parents is going to include "fix it and you" or "destroy any ambition and desire." No, self-care for parents must be Christ-centered, lifting up the weary head, and be both practical and spiritual, which is where the Holy Spirit does His work within Christ's Bride—the Church. I don't purport that every parent is going to resonate with our self-care strategy, but I do hope that in some way, it does encourage wherever you may be on your parenting journey. I believe that first and foremost self-care for parents is Christ-care for parents, resting entirely in the truth of God's Word, remembering the atonement on our behalf which brings peace beyond understanding, and knowing our identity in Christ—that we are loved, cared for, fully known, and eternally written into the palms of our loving God. Peace comes in the acknowledgment of ourselves and the acknowledgment of our children within the context of the gospel.

Community Support and Resources
Find a Like-Minded Community for Support
The Christ-centered approach to raising children is not a common one in many Western cultures. As we look to support parents in their desire to lead their households in grace and point their children to Christ, having a community to share ideas, experiences, and resources with is imperative. Seek other families that are interested in this same approach to parenting. Connect with other parents at church, in your community, sports, and schools. Attend Train Up a Child! Conferences and other biblically-based parenting events as available. Included below are groups of other parents who have committed to starting parenting small groups using the material of Grace in Parenting and The Prayer of a Parent. If you are near any of these groups, you are welcome to join in. For those who are looking for what to say to other parents, here is some text that you can copy and paste into an email or text to begin the conversation:

Parenting is tough and can be one of the most rewarding positions. Many parents out there struggle as to how to parent and discipline their children, my husband and I are no exception. We are parents who are looking to build our family on biblical principles, increasing the level of Christ-likeness in our home. The material we have been using speaks to this and we invite and encourage you to consider joining us. We want to reach as many families as we can, not to tell you that we have all the answers, but to share with you what others have already shared with us. Would you like to be a part of this community in addition to us?

CHAPTER 9

Conclusion

We have emphasized both the methods and goals of peaceful parenting as a Christ-centered pursuit of the virtues. In the introduction, we made the case for orienting peaceful parenting around the growth in virtue that accompanies growing in grace. We emphasized the imitative aspects of virtue, and so encouraged parents to prioritize the formation of their own souls. In part one, we called attention to the philosophical and psychological obstacles to the idea that virtues can be formed, and suggested that a biblical view of humanity could powerfully undermine these obstacles. In part two, we offered a biblical virtue ethics as a means of not only forming the virtues, but orienting parents toward the love of Christ and the imitation of his character. In part three, we detailed the ways that each of the virtues we discussed in part two could be approached as goals of peaceful parenting, in order to give parents a sense of what peaceful parenting could look like in practice. And in the first chapter of part four, we described resources and principles of peaceful parenting that were not described or discussed in the earlier parts of the book, but that seem to also be an outworking of part one's and part two's emphasis on the parent's own virtue formation—an emphasis we are eager to reinforce.

In this conclusion, we want to give final encouragements to the parent eager to approach discipleship with her children in a way that is focused first on her growth in grace. We intend to move through the virtues a final time, though with some differences not just in what we say but how we say it. Each of the subsections of this conclusion addresses exactly one of the virtues of part two.

Recap of Key Points
1. God is sovereign, gracious, and utterly committed to our good. 2. In every situation, God always gives us the grace we need to deal with conflict in Christlike ways. 3. If we would realize the oneness God has established for Christians with Himself and with each other, it would make it easier to face issues and solve them. 4. Conflict either brings us together or pulls us apart. 5. What does the will of God look like concerning children's behavior? 6. The key to solomonic learning is that the father is characterized by graciousness. 7. Grace actually grows people. We parents need grace. Our children need grace. Our children need to see grace from us. 8. Sometimes we must be very firm with our children, and a very determined will must be used when dealing with them. 9. Examine yourself. If you are not successful in maintaining peace in your home, examine yourself.

We have now finished this little book about growing in grace instead of manners-centered or child-centered discipline. We have tried to demonstrate that Christ Himself, living in the hearts of His people, through the power of the Holy Spirit and His Word, will produce peace, love, joy, righteousness, sanctification, and self-discipline. Therefore, He will produce graciousness in the heart of a Christian parent. It is our desire that we will all evaluate our parenting because the fulfillment of the Commandment, "Honor your father and your mother," is fully answered in "Love is the fulfillment of law." Parenting in this fashion will promote unity, happiness, and love among family members. Let's remember, sin disrupts relationships. We were committed to continual selfishness. Children must be trained to develop committed faithfulness. The mother is a vice-regent of God in the home. Just remember, what the kids do that bugs us is most likely the very attitudes and behaviors that God is using to reveal our hearts-divider treatment.

Encouragement for the Parenting Journey

You have been given a high calling with the gift of a child. The Lord loves your child more than you can imagine. You have been called to be the nurturing hands and feet of Christ to your child. Through the experiences you provide, your child learns how to live. Please know that we are also walking this path. We do not write from a parenting pedestal, but instead we speak from hearts full of hopes and dreams for our children. We are learning and relearning how to love Jesus and how to love all those who cross our path, no matter how short their legs may be. Grace washes over every step in this process. Somehow we know that the Lord uses all of our mistakes and messes to bless our children with the perfect love of Christ.

It is natural to compare. Relationships—especially those with children—surround us. Children look different, learn at varying rates, and have vastly different personalities. Even siblings often contrast greatly. We are human, and we compare. Food consumption is an easy area to compare. Does your child eat? How much does your child consume? Peaceful Parenting encourages you to stop. Stop measuring your child's blessings against those of another. Consider eliminating labels from your speech. These terms often end up using your child rather than describing your child. Labels should not define who your children grow up to be. Avoid setting life limitations on your children. We cannot see the future, but our heavenly Father has blessed each of His children with a unique array of abilities and personalities. Guide your children. Provide them with balanced meals and opportunities to engage in physical movement. Host a family bike ride, sign up for swim lessons, and plan an occasional hike or two. Do not exercise with the sole goal of weight loss or management.

www.ingramcontent.com/pod-product-compliance
Lightning Source LLC
LaVergne TN
LVHW041642070526
838199LV00053B/3507